Little Children's Bible Books

DANIEL

Retold by Anne de Graaf
Illustrated by José Pérez Montero

BROADMAN
&HOLMAN
PUBLISHERS

DANIEL

Published in 1999 by Broadman & Holman Publishers,
Nashville, Tennessee

Text copyright © 1998 Anne de Graaf
Illustration copyright © 1998 José Pérez Montero
Design by Ben Alex
Conceived, designed and produced by
Scandinavia Publishing House

Printed in Hong Kong
ISBN 0-8054-1898-9

Dedicated to José Pérez Montero's grandchildren and to Daniël de Graaf

A long, long time ago, there was a young boy who was different. He was very brave and very clever. Some say he was a prince of Jerusalem. His name was Daniel.

7

During a terrible war, an enemy
army attacked Jerusalem and took
many of God's people prisoner.
Poor Daniel! The soldiers marched
him off to Babylon, far away.

Daniel was determined never to forget his home or his family. Now he was trapped like an animal in a cage. What did Daniel do? He talked to God.

The king of Babylon was called
Nebuchadnezzar. He ordered the
soldiers to search through the many
prisoners. "Look for the strongest
and cleverest boys. Then send them
to my special school!"

*Can you say
"Nebuchadnezzar"?
Not with your
mouth full! Where
is the king?*

10

11

At the king's special school Daniel and his friends had to read Babylonian and write Babylonian.

They even had new Babylonian names. Daniel was called "Belteshazzar." How do you say THAT?

They had to eat like Babylonians, drink like Babylonians, and pray like Babylonians. Finally, Daniel told his teachers, "No! We're not like you. We're different."

Daniel told his friends, "Remember who we are! We're different than the Babylonians. Remember what our parents taught us!"

Daniel and his friends were trying to follow God's rules for his people. Name one thing your parents have taught YOU.

"What do you mean different?
Follow the king's orders. Eat and
drink what we do!" the guards
told Daniel.

Daniel said, "No. Then we will be
breaking God's rules for our people
about healthy living. Please, let us
eat just vegetables and water!"

God warmed the heart of Daniel's teacher. "Daniel, if the king finds out about this, he'll have me killed. What do I tell him when you grow skinny and weak?"

Ten days later Daniel's teacher was amazed! Daniel and his friends were in much better shape than the other boys.

God gave Daniel an idea. Daniel said, "I know! Let there be a contest. Give us vegetables and water for ten days. When you see how God makes us stronger and healthier than the others, the king can't punish you."

Do you eat YOUR vegetables?

And they had gained more weight than the other boys! Daniel's teacher agreed to let them follow God's rules instead of the king's.

Let's see your tummy. Is it as full as mine?

And for the next three years, God blessed the boys so they grew big and strong.

How tall are you? Do you have a special place where someone can measure how fast you grow? Go check it now.

Many years later, during the reign of King Belshazzar, he saw a strange hand write something on his wall.

What happens if YOU write on the wall? Who's not happy?

28

The king could not read what was
on the wall. So he sent for Daniel.
Daniel prayed and God showed
him what it meant.

Sometimes we don't know what something means. Talking to God always helps us look at things differently.

31

When Daniel was an old man, his enemies tricked the king and had Daniel arrested. "You must

Poor Daniel, a prisoner again. What did Daniel do this time? He talked to God.

punish him for praying to his God," these enemies told the king.

The guards threw Daniel into a pit
with lions! But God sent an angel to
shut the lions' mouths. Daniel stayed
there all night.

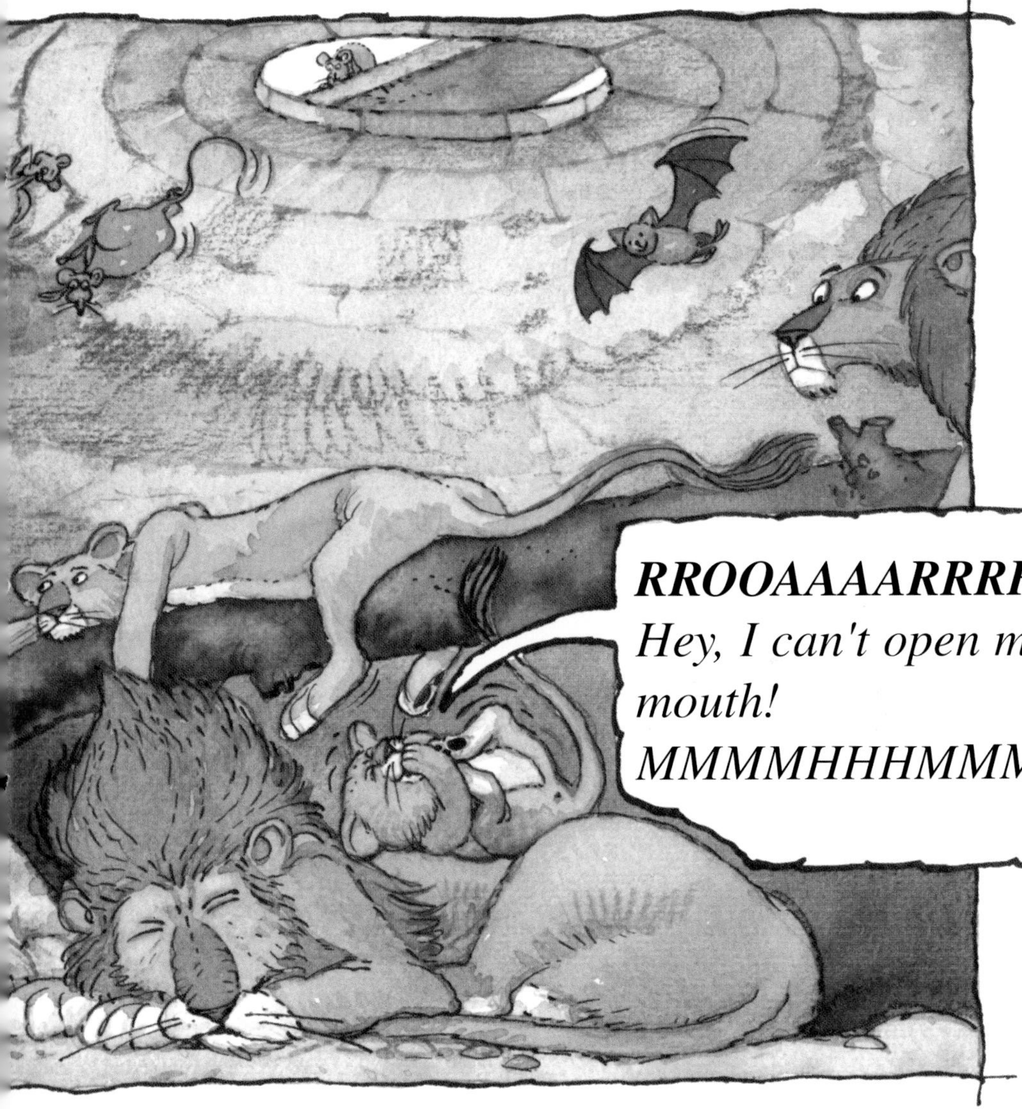
RROOAAAARRRR!
Hey, I can't open my mouth!
MMMMHHHMMM!

In the morning Daniel did not even have one scratch on him. "God kept me safe," he told the king.

Why was Daniel different? What did he do at least three times every day, no matter if it landed him with the lions? Daniel talked to God! Did YOU talk to God today?

A NOTE TO THE big PEOPLE:

The *Little Children's Bible Books* may be your child's first introduction to the Bible, God's Word. This story makes the book of Daniel spring to life. This is a DO book. Point things out, ask your child to find, seek, say, and discover.

Before you read these stories, pray that your child's little heart would be touched by the love of God. These stories are about planting seeds, having vision, learning right from wrong, choosing to believe.

Daniel is one of the first steps on the way. The Bible story is told in straight type.

A LITTLE something fun is said in italics by the narrating animal to make the story come alive. In this DO book, wave, wink, hop, roar or do any of the other things the stories suggest so this can become a fun time of growing closer.

Pray together after you read this. There's no better way for big people to learn from little people.